SOUTH COAST RAILWAYS ~

BRIGHTON

TO

EASTBOURNE

Vic Mitchell and Keith Smith

Published to commemorate the
golden jubilee of electric
traction on the route.

First published 1985

ISBN 0 906520 16 9

© Middleton Press, 1985

Phototypeset by   CitySet Ltd, Chichester.

Published by   Middleton Press
              Easebourne Lane
              Midhurst, West Sussex.
              GU29 9AZ

Printed & bound by   Diddles Ltd.,
                    Guildford and Kings Lynn.

CONTENTS

ACKNOWLEDGMENTS

We would like to express our sincere thanks to all those mentioned in the caption credits, many of whom have kindly supplied detailed information. We are also very grateful to D. Clayton, Mrs. E. Fisk, N. Langridge, R. Randell, N. Stanyon and our wives for their help.

GEOGRAPHICAL SETTING

The coast between Brighton and Eastbourne is almost entirely composed of high chalk cliffs, which form the eastern end of the South Downs. It was necessary therefore for this part of the South Coast Railway to be built inland, behind the Downs. The line from London had been built along the side of the broad shallow valley in which Brighton is situated. This valley was the first obstacle to be crossed, by means of a viaduct. The summit of the Downs was penetrated by a tunnel.

Lewes is situated in one of the few river gaps in the South Downs and was of importance strategically and as a market town. The River Ouse formed a valley ideal for road and rail but both soon leave it to run parallel to the northern escarpment of the Downs. The final few miles of the route are along the side of the Willingdon Levels.

The Ordnance Survey maps reproduced in this album are to the scale of 25 miles to 1 inch.

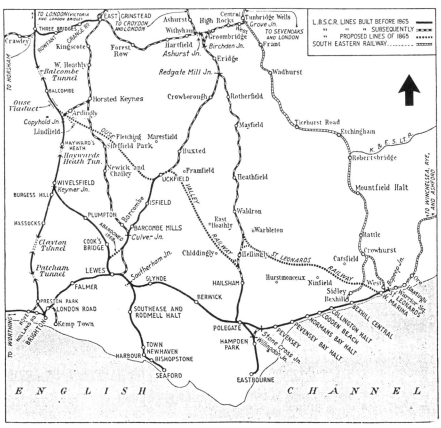

(Railway Magazine)

HISTORICAL BACKGROUND

The line between London and Brighton was opened in 1841 and the East Coast line to Lewes followed on 8th June 1846, together with one intermediate station near Falmer. On June 27th of the same year, it was extended almost to Hastings, with a station at Polegate serving South Bourne and its less significant neighbour, East Bourne. A less heavily engineered branch from the London main line at Keymer junction (south of Haywards Heath) was opened to Lewes on 1st October 1847. A branch northwards from the line was opened to Uckfield in October 1858 but was realigned on a more direct route into Lewes on 1st October 1868.

Newhaven received rail connection in 1847 and branches to Eastbourne and Hailsham were brought into use on 14th May 1849. The latter was extended northwards to Tunbridge Wells on 1st September 1880. The local network was completed on 2nd August 1871 when a spur was opened to permit direct running between Eastbourne and Hastings.

Through running from Eastbourne to Tunbridge Wells ceased on 14th June 1965 although a shuttle service to Hailsham was retained until 9th September 1968.

The complications over the closure of the Lewes to East Grinstead line are detailed in our *Branch Lines to East Grinstead*, services being finally withdrawn in 1958.

The Lewes to Uckfield link was closed in 1969. The lines included in this album were electrified on 7th July 1935, with exception of the Kemp Town branch, the brief history of which is given adjacent to photograph no. 24.

1957

From NORTH to SOUTH		From SOUTH to NORTH	
	pm		am
SHEFFIELD (Victoria) .. .. .. dep	11 G 44F	HASTINGS .. .. dep	10A 20
	am	ST. LEONARDS (Warrior Square) ,,	10A 24
CHESTERFIELD CENTRAL .. .. ,,	12 13	ST. LEONARDS (West Marina) .. ,,	10 28
NOTTINGHAM (Victoria) .. .. ,,	1 B 7	BEXHILL (Central) .. .. ,,	10A 36
LOUGHBOROUGH (Central) .. ,,	1 30	EASTBOURNE .. .. ,,	10 A 42
LEICESTER (Central) .. .. .. ,,	1 50	Seaford .. .. ,,	10 C 44
Rugby (Central) .. .. ,,	2 21	BRIGHTON .. .. ,,	11 38
Woodford Halse .. .. ,,	2 46		
BRIGHTON .. .. arr	6 4		pm
Seaford .. .. ,,	7 C 7	Woodford Halse .. .. arr	3 9
EASTBOURNE .. .. ,,	6 51	Rugby (Central) .. .. ,,	3 33
BEXHILL (Central) .. .. ,,	7 20	LEICESTER (Central) .. .. .. ,,	4 1
ST. LEONARDS (West Marina) .. ,,	7 27	LOUGHBOROUGH (Central) .. ,,	4 19
ST. LEONARDS (Warrior Square) ,,	7 31	NOTTINGHAM (Victoria) .. .. ,,	4D 39
HASTINGS .. .. ,,	7 35	SHEFFIELD (Victoria) .. .. .. ,,	5 45

A Seats may be reserved at a fee of 1/- per seat upon personal or postal request to the Station Master. Early application is advisable
B Connecting service available from Derby (friargate) dep 11F35 pm, Ilkeston North dep 11F54 pm, Kimberley East dep 12 3 am

C Change at Brighton
D Connecting service available to Basford North, Kimberley East, Ilkeston North, Derby (Friargate), and Chesterfield Central

F Friday nights 28th June to 6th September
G Note "A" applies except on 26th July and 2nd August

THROUGH TRAINS BETWEEN

BIRKENHEAD, WOLVERHAMPTON, BIRMINGHAM,

AND

RAMSGATE, FOLKESTONE, BRIGHTON, HASTINGS,

Via Reading.

Left Table

	Week Days			Suns.	
	a.m.	a.m.	a.m.	a.m.	
Liverpool (Central, Low Level) ¶..dep.	6 19	...	7 45	...	
Liverpool (Landing Stage) ¶ "	6 15	...	7 40	...	
Birkenhead (Woodside) ¶ "	6 30	...	8 0	...	
Chester "	7 8	...	8 35	...	
Wrexham "	7 37	...	8 56	...	
Shrewsbury "	8 40	...	9 43	8 55	
Wolverhampton (Low Level) "	9 45	10 20	10 30	12 20	
Kidderminster "	9 20	10 2	10 12	10 25	
Birmingham (Snow Hill) "	10 20	10 45	10 55	12 55	
Warwick "	10 1	11 2	11 2	1 10	
Leamington Spa "	10 47	11 15	11 25	1 25	
				a.m.	
L.N.E. Railway — Sheffield (Victoria) "	5 2	7 30	7 30	9 15	
Nottingham (Victoria) "	7 36	8 48	8 48	10 14	
Leicester (Central) "	8 13	9 35	9 35	10 53	
Rugby (Central) "	8 42	10 13	10 13	11 11	
				p.m.	
Banbury "	11 12	11 17	11 53	1 52	
	a.m.	a.m.	a.m.	a.m.	
Malvern (Great) dep.	8 35	8 25	8 25		
Worcester (Shrub Hill) "	9 5	9 5	9 5		
Evesham "	9 29	9 29	9 29	11 8	
				p.m.	
Oxford "	11 44	12 18	12 25	2 27	
Reading arr.	12 14	12 53	1 0		
		a.m.	a.m.	a.m.	
Plymouth (North Road) dep.	...	8 42	8 42	7 55	
Torquay "	...	8 42	8 42	9 9	
Exeter (St. David's) "	7 55	10 0	10 0	9 17	
Taunton "	9 40	10 45	10 45	10 23	
Bristol (Temple Meads) "	9 58	9 58	9 58	12 50	
Bath "	9 58	9 58	9 58	12 53	
Chippenham "	10 19	10 19	10 19	9 40	
Weymouth "	9 0	9 0	9 0	9 40	
Yeovil (Pen Mill) "	9 51	9 51	9 51	9 41	
Swansea (High Street) "	7 0	7 0	6 45	9 5	
Cardiff (General) "	8 15	8 15	8 15	11 0	
Newport dep.	8 35	8 35	8 25	11 20	
Hereford "	7 35	7 35	7 55	9 25	
Cheltenham Spa (St. James') "	9 20	9 20	9 20	10 3500	
Gloucester "	9 43	9 43	9 43	9 50	
Stroud "	10 2	10 2	10 2	9 35	
Swindon "	10 52	10 52	10 52	1 45	
Reading arr.	12 10	12 38	12 38	2 44	
		p.m.	p.m.	p.m.	
Reading (G.W.R. Station) dep.	12 15	12 50	1 10 1 10	3 5	
North Camp arr.	...	1 21	1 41 1 41	3 36	
Guildford "	1 0	1 38	1 58 1 56	3 50	
Redhill "	1 35	2 33	2 33 2 40	4 20	
Brighton "	2 15	3 5	3 25 3 33	5 25	
	p.m.	p.m.	p.m.	p.m.	
Hove arr.	2 23	3 20	3 37 3 50	5 37	
Shoreham-by-Sea "	2 33	3 27	3 50 3 57	5 40	
Worthing Central "	2 41	3 35	4 14 5	6 13	
Littlehampton "	3 7	4 0	4 32 4 32	6 30	
Bognor Regis "	2 45	3 28	4 24 4 24	5 45	
Lewes "	2 56	3 49	4 11 4 28	5 56	
Newhaven Town "	2 57	3 50	4 34 4 35	6 1	
Newhaven Harbour "	3 3	3 56	4 34 4 41	6 5	
Seaford "	2 57	3 53	4 38 4 43	6 5	
Eastbourne "	3 23	4 18	4 54 4 50	6 52	
Bexhill Central "	3 35	4 47	4 49 4 58	6 48	
St. Leonards (West Marina) "	3 35	4 47	4 49 4 58	6 49	
St. Leonards (Warrior Square) "	3 40	4 51	4 53 4 58	6 54	
Hastings "	3 40	4 51	4 53 4 58	6 54	
	p.m.	p.m.	p.m.	p.m.	
Tonbridge arr.	2[33	2 40	3 5 3 18	5 0	
Ashford (Kent) "	...	3 22	3 36 4 0	5 33	
Canterbury West "	...	3 48	4 7	6 5	
Minster Jctn. (Thanet) "	...	4 7	4 23 4 33	6 23	
Ramsgate "	...	4 20	4 33	6 33	
Dumpton Park "	...	4 25	4 40	6 48	
Broadstairs "	...	4 29	4 44	6 56	
Margate "	...	4 38	4 53	6 5	
Shorncliffe "	...	...	5 56 5510	6 9	
Folkestone Central "	...	...	3 59 4 20	6 27	
Dover Priory "	...	...	4 13 4 34	6 27	
Martin Mill "	...	...	4 27 4 49	6 43	
Walmer "	...	...	4 33 4 55	6 49	
Deal "	...	...	4 38 5 0	6 54	
Sandwich "	...	...	4[49 5 11		

Right Table

	Week Days			Suns.	
	a.m.	a.m.	p.m.	a.m.	
Sandwich dep.	...	9 13		10 39	
Deal "	...	9 23		10 50	
Walmer "	...	9 28		10 55	
Martin Mill "	...	9 35		11 2	
Dover Priory "	...	9 48		11 15	
Folkestone Central "	...	10 8		11 35	
Shorncliffe "	...	10 11		11 38	
Margate "	9 20	9[20		10 40	
Broadstairs "	9 29	9S27		10 49	
Dumpton Park "	9 33	9S31		10 53	
Ramsgate "	9 33	9S36		11 0	
Minster Jctn. (Thanet) "	9 46	9X44		11 10	
Canterbury West "	10 5	10Sr3		11 28	
Ashford (Kent) "	...	10 33		12 0	
Tonbridge "	10 57	11 8		12 35	
	a.m.	a.m.	p.m.	a.m.	
Hastings dep.	9 5	9A25	12 18	10 45	
St. Leonards (Warrior Square) "	9 8	9A27	12 22	10 47	
St. Leonards (West Marina) "	8 49	9S032	12 26	10 54	
Bexhill Central "	9 15	9A35	12 35	10 54	
Eastbourne "	9 42	10 A5	12 52	11 33	
Seaford "	9 42	9 44	12 9	11 21	
Newhaven Harbour "	9 46	9 49	12 32	11 19	
Newhaven Town "	9 51	9 51	12 54	11 22	
Lewes "	10 2	10 18	1 5	11 47	
Bognor Regis "	9 10	9 44	12 36	11 19	
Littlehampton "	9 28	9 59	12 36	11 19	
Worthing Central "	9 44	10 17	12 52	11 48	
Shoreham-by-Sea "	9 56	10 25	1 3	11 56	
Hove "	10 3	10 33	1 16	12 3	
		a.m.	p.m.	p.m.	
Brighton dep.	10 25	10 45	1 33	12 15	
Redhill "	11 28	11 40	2 28	1 8	
		p.m.	p.m.	p.m.	
Guildford "	12 5	12 15	2 54	1 42	
North Camp "	12 21	12 31		1 56	
Reading (G.W.R. Station) arr.	12 55	12 55	3 38	2 20	
	p.m.	p.m.	p.m.	p.m.	
Reading dep.	1 5	1 5	3 45	2 30	
Oxford arr.	1 25	1 38	4 30	3 17	
Evesham "	4 13	4 13	6 50	7 27	
Worcester (Shrub Hill) "	4 37	4 37	7 17	7 55	
Malvern (Great) "	4 58	4 58	7 34	8 26	
	p.m.	p.m.	p.m.	p.m.	
Reading dep.	1 17		6 8	5 20	
Yeovil (Pen Mill) arr.	3 20		8 5	5 20	
Weymouth "	4 8		10 0	6 8	
	p.m.	p.m.	p.m.	p.m.	
Reading dep.	1 17	1 17	6 8	5 20	
Swindon arr.	3 4	3 4	4 43	5 28	
Stroud "	3 37	3 37	5 37	5 55	
Gloucester "	4 44	4 44	5 57	6 14	
Cheltenham Spa (St. James') "	5 15	5 15	6 14	6 26	
Hereford "	6850		8 12		
Newport "	4 32	4 32	7 38	7 37	
Cardiff (General) "	5 57	5 57	7 58	8 47	
Swansea (High Street) "	6 19	6 19	9 43	8[41	
Chippenham "	3 35	3 35	5 30	6 2	
Bath "	3 54	3 54	6 18	5V24	
Bristol (Temple Meads) "	4 15	4 15	6 27	F5V45	
	p.m.	p.m.	p.m.	p.m.	
Taunton dep.	2 20	2 20	4 58	3 16	
Exeter (St. David's) arr.	4[12	4 12	6 0	4 58	
Torquay "	...	4 58	9 49	6 10	
Plymouth (North Road) "	...	6 1	10 25	7 45	
	p.m.	p.m.	p.m.	p.m.	
Reading dep.	1 5	1 5	3 45	2 30	
Banbury arr.	2 0	2 13	4 53	3 40	
L.N.E. Railway — Rugby (Central) "	...	3 47	6 50	4 47	
Leicester (Central) "	...	4 11	7 49	5 48	
Nottingham (Victoria) "	...	4 45	7 49	6 33	
Sheffield (Victoria) "	...	5 40	9424	6 39	
Leamington Spa "	2 31	2 39	5 22	4 6	
Warwick "	2 59	2 59	5 54	4 5	
Birmingham (Snow Hill) "	3 0	3 10	5 55	4 35	
Kidderminster "	4 18	4 18	7 20	5 41	
Wolverhampton (Low Level) "	3 25	3 35	6 22	5 27	
Shrewsbury "	4 53	4 22	7 21	6 9	
Ruabon "	5 4	5 4	8 21	6 50	
Wrexham "	5 14	5 14	8 15	7 0	
Chester "	5 35	5 35	8 34	7 21	
Birkenhead (Woodside) ‡ "	6 16	6 16	9 10	8 0	
Liverpool (Landing Stage) ‡ "	6 27	6 27	9 27	8 17	
Liverpool (Central, Low Level) "	6 22	6 22	9 18	8 18	

A Seats in compartments may be reserved, 1/- per seat. Application, with fee, to reach Station Master before 40 p.m. day prior to the journey. a Also due Sandwich 4 38 p.m. by changing Minster Jctn. (Thanet).   B Via Worcester.   b Change at Ashford (Kent).   C Slip Carriage.
D Via Honeybourne.   d On Saturdays, July 9th and 16th and Sept. 10th, arrives Sheffield 9 38 p.m   F Stapleton Road.   G Change at Redhill.
H Also dep. Sandwich 9SO29 a.m., changing Minster Jctn. (Thanet).   J On Saturdays, Reading dep 1 17 p.m.   K Also dep Sandwich 10 59 a.m. changing Minster Jctn. (Thanet).   SO Saturdays only.   SX Saturdays excepted.   V Via Westbury.   Reading dep. 3 16 p.m
Y Reading dep. 4 40 p.m.   Z Reading dep. 3 16 p.m

† Malvern Road Station. St. James' arr. 5 26 p.m. (5 41 p.m. on Sats.).   § 15 mins. later on Sats.

¶ The departures from Liverpool (Landing Stage) are by the Liverpool and Birkenhead Ferry Steamers to Birkenhead (Woodside). Trains start alongside the Quay. Passengers from Liverpool (Central, Low Level) travel by the Mersey Railway and change at Rock Ferry.

‡ The arrivals at Liverpool (Landing Stage) are by the Birkenhead and Liverpool Ferry Steamers from Birkenhead (Woodside). Trains run alongside the Quay. Passengers for Liverpool (Central, Low Level) change at Rock Ferry to the Mersey Railway.

PASSENGER SERVICES

The May 1847 service consisted of five trains each way on weekdays and two on Sundays. By June 1869, there was an additional train on weekdays from Brighton to Seaford and also one to Hastings, with an extra journey to Lewes on Tuesdays only. A more frequent service of branch line trains was operated between Polegate and Eastbourne, to give connections to and from both up and down main line trains.

From 1st April 1884, the South Eastern Railway started a twice-daily express service between Eastbourne and London (Charing Cross) via Hailsham, Eridge and Tunbridge Wells. It was not a success and was withdrawn at the end of the following year.

In 1890, there were fifteen through trains between Brighton and Eastbourne on weekdays (three on Sundays) with an additional six (four on Sundays) west of Lewes. These figures exclude a number of through trains direct to London.

After years of agitation, Eastbourne obtained a through service to the Midlands and the North, via Brighton, Clapham Junction and Willesden junction.

It commenced on 23rd July 1904 and carried coaches for Liverpool (Lime Street), Manchester (London Road) and Birmingham (New Street), together with dining cars. The imaginative name of *Sunny South Express* was applied to this train for many decades.

There were only minor changes to the time tables during the early years of this century, such as the provision of a 5.10 pm departure from Lewes for Glynde and Berwick, on Tuesdays only.

Electrification of the route in 1935 brought the introduction of a regular interval service, the basic pattern of which was two stopping trains per hour between Brighton and Ore and between Brighton and Seaford, with a fast train hourly between London and Hastings which included a Pullman or Pantry car. A non-stop all Pullman electric train ran on summer Sundays, reviving an LBSCR practice.

World War II brought about some temporary reduction in services and withdrawal of catering services, but little change occurred until 1965-66 when the London trains were terminated at Eastbourne and one of the hourly Seaford trains withdrawn. Subsequent cut backs reduced the service to only two trains per hour on any part of the route although a 20-minute interval was restored to Lewes-Brighton section due mainly to the increase in traffic to and from the University of Sussex at Falmer.

Inter-regional services recommenced in

NORTH TO SOUTH					SOUTH TO NORTH				
		Fridays & Sats. only	Sats. only				Fridays & Sats. only	Sats. only	
		a.m.	p.m.				a.m.	a.m.	
Birmingham (New St.) dep.		11A 40	...	Hastings ... ... dep.			10A 45	10A 51	
Coventry ... ... ,,		p.m. 12 8	...	St. Leonards (W. Sq.) ,,			10A 48	10A 55	
Leicester (L.M.R.) ... ,,		...	12A 30	St. Leonards (W. M.) ,,			10 52	10 59	
Market Harboro' ... ... ,,	Restaurant Car Train, Birmingham to Hastings	...	Through Train, Leicester to Hastings	1 7	Bexhill (Central) ... ... ,,	Restaurant Car Train, Hastings to Birmingham	10A 59	Through Train, Hastings to Leicester	11A 7
Northampton (Castle) ... ,,		...		1 48	Eastbourne ... ... ,,		11A 29		11A 37
East Croydon ... ... arr.		2 27		3 54	Brighton ... ... ,,		p.m. 12 13		p.m. 12 27
Brighton ... ... ,,		3 25		4 55	East Croydon ... ... ,,		1 10		1 17
Eastbourne ... ... ,,		4 8		5 45	Northampton (Castle) ... arr.		...		3 17
Bexhill (Central) ... ... ,,		4 38		6 10	Market Harboro' ... ... ,,		...		3 54
St. Leonards (W. M.) ,,		4 45		6 17	Leicester (L.M.R.) ... ,,		...		4 23
St. Leonards (W. Sq.) ,,		4 49		6 21	Coventry ... ... ,.		3 27		...
Hastings ... ... ,,		4 54		6 25	Birmingham (New St.) ,,		4 0		...

1949

A—Seats can be reserved, 1/- per seat.

the summer of 1949, after an absence of 10 years, with a train to Birmingham on Fridays and Saturdays and Leicester on Saturdays. In 1951, the Birkenhead train was restored, running every weekday throughout the year. During the 1950s, holiday travel by rail reached its peak, through trains also reaching Eastbourne from Walsall, Sheffield and Wolverhampton. By the mid-1960s, regular through trains had ceased to run north of the Thames.

NORTH TO SOUTH

	Fridays only	Saturdays only	Saturdays only
	p.m.	a.m.	p.m.
Manchester (London Road) ... ... dep.	11 A 40	...	...
Stockport (Edgeley) ... ... ,,	11 58	...	...
Stoke-on-Trent ... ... ,	a.m. 1 10	...	...
Walsall ... ... ,,	...	11A 5	...
Birmingham (New Street) ... ... ,,	...	11A 40	...
Coventry ... ... ,,	...	p.m. 12 8	...
Leicester (London Road) ... ... ,,	...	...	12A 35
Market Harborough ... ... ,,	...	...	1 7
Northampton (Castle) ... ... ,,	...	...	1 48
East Croydon ... ... arr.	...	2 26	3 53
Brighton	5B 46	3 23	4 55
Seaford ... ... ,,	7BC7	4C 11	6 C 5
Eastbourne ... ... ,,	6B 32	4 6	5 45
Bexhill (Central) ... ... ,,	6B 59	4 37	6 10
St. Leonards (West Marina) ... ... ,,	7B 6	4 44	6 17
St. Leonards (Warrior Square) ... ... ,,	7B 10	4 48	6 21
Hastings ... ... ,,	7B 14	4 52	6 25

Column notes (Fridays only): Through Train, Manchester (London Rd.) to Hastings 2nd July to 3rd September only
Column notes (Saturdays only a.m.): Through Train, Walsall to Hastings 3rd July to 4th September only
Column notes (Saturdays only p.m.): Through Train, Leicester to Hastings 3rd July to 4th September only

SOUTH TO NORTH

	Saturdays only	Saturdays only	Saturdays only
	a.m.	a.m.	p.m.
Hastings ... ... dep.	10A 45	10A 51	12A 30
St. Leonards (Warrior Square) ... ... ,,	10A 49	10A 55	12A 34
St. Leonards (West Marina) ... ... ,,	10 54	10 59	12 38
Bexhill (Central) ... ... ,,	11A 2	11A 7	12A 47
Eastbourne ... ... ,,	11A 30	11A 39	12A 55
Seaford ... ... ,,	11C 23	11C 44	12C 44
Brighton ... ... ,,	p.m. 12 15	p.m. 12 27	1 50
East Croydon ... ... ,,	1 10	1 17	...
Northampton (Castle) ... ... arr.	...	3 12	...
Market Harborough ... ... ,,	...	3 49	...
Leicester (London Road) ... ... ,,	...	4 23	...
Coventry ... ... ,,	3 25	...	...
Birmingham (New Street) ... ... ,,	4 1	...	...
Walsall ... ... ,,	4 26	...	...
Stoke-on-Trent ... ... ,,	...	...	6 13
Stockport (Edgeley) ... ... ,,	...	...	7 0
Manchester (London Road) ... ... ,,	...	...	7 16

Column notes (1st): Through Train, Hastings to Walsall 3rd July to 4th September only
Column notes (2nd): Through Train, Hastings to Leicester 3rd July to 4th September only
Column notes (3rd): Through Train, Hastings to Manchester (London Rd.) 3rd July to 4th September only

1954

A—Seats can be reserved, 1/- per seat. C—Change at Brighton.

BRIGHTON

1. The clock and balustrade are above the frontage of the original terminus. The buildings were designed by David Mocatta and constructed in 1840-41. The porte-cochere (cab road cover) and the train shed were later additions, whilst the Terminus Hotel was an early loss due to road widening. (D. Cullum collection)

2. An Edwardian picture postcard view of the interior. It is noon in high summer and some of the ladies have parasols, even within the shade of the station roof. On the right is a local 'growler' or '4-wheeler' with its roof down for hot weather and behind it, a B4 class 4-4-0 stands at the buffer stops. At this time the present platform 7 was numbered 4, and numbers 5 and 6 were called 3. The station roof is being painted and no less than three immense ladders can be seen, each of which looks perilous in the extreme. (Lens of Sutton)

3. A truly suburban service was operated to Kemp Town, usually from the most easterly platform of the terminus (latterly no. 10). Here we see the smoke of no. 73, one of the Terrier class, drifting over the incredibly ornate canopy valance, sometime before 1919 when the locomotive was withdrawn. (E.R. Lacey collection)

4. A Terrier in Stroudley livery reverses past an array of signal counterweights, apparently under the guidance of a bowler-hatted official. The route indicator 'B' denotes the use of the second (from the east) of five reversible running lines at the approach to the station. The cylinder hanging from the pole in the centre of the picture is a self adjusting arc light, known as a Jablachkoff candle.
(Lens of Sutton)

6. An Uckfield line train leaving platform 10 at Brighton in June 1953 with a double domed C2X class no. 32440 in charge of an SE&CR 'Birdcage' set. Alongside is 2NOL electric set no. 1834, made up of L&SWR steam carriage bodies on SR underframes, which will soon leave for Ore via Eastbourne. On the right is the station pilot no. 32169, an E3 class 0–6–2 tank. The office on the left is part of the locomotive works, now demolished and, together with platform 10, swallowed up in the present station car park. (P. Hay)

5. On the right of this view (and the previous one) is the works in which most of the earlier locomotives seen in this album were built. No. B644, hauling one of two prototype Balloon coaches, forms the railmotor from Kemp Town as it clatters past the lofty wall of the works. Three other moving engines help to emphasise the bustle at this complex location in steam days. (J.E. Kite)

7. The 8.55 am to Tonbridge leaving Brighton behind class L no. 31760, in May 1959. Just behind the train is the McKenzie & Holland signal gantry which was retained as a staff footbridge, while the brick building with the round-headed windows was once the base of Brighton Montpelier Junction signal box. Steam in the distance rises over the loco shed and the chalk cliff beside the West Coast line is just visible beyond. In the left foreground is one of the 1932 Westinghouse 2-aspect colour light ground signals, controlling exit from the siding. (P. Hay)

8. One of the venerable old 2BIL sets, with a battered corner, is seen Lewes-bound in platform 8 in the winter of 1968-69. The SR headcode 16 was used to Ore and 28 to Seaford. In platform 9, we see a class 33 diesel locomotive at the head of a Victoria via Uckfield train. (J.A.M. Vaughan)

9. Part of the fascination of Brighton station is the engineering of the train sheds on a curve. Another interesting feature is the relatively simple roof span over the east coast lines. Furthermore, platform 9 is largely of timber construction as it is suspended above the valley, into the side of which the station site has been cut and built up.
(Lens of Sutton)

10. The fine curved bracings of one of the two main spans of the 1882 roof are best seen from a high level, but the tastefully redecorated stanchions can be enjoyed from the platform. The twice daily through trains to Manchester via Reading usually use platform 7. The traditional collection and delivery of parcels ceased in June 1981. (A.A.F. Bell)

12. Although usually known as London Road Viaduct, the part of the London road it crosses is in fact called Preston Road, as this Edwardian post card correctly records. The structure has 27 arches with a maximum height of 67 feet. It is 400 yards long with a minimum curve of 10 chains. Its 10 million bricks were laid in a mere 10 months in 1845-46. (Lens of Sutton)

11. This regretfully undated view across the fields north of Brighton shows two carriage sheds on either side of the Lewes line. A map of 1873 shows only sidings on their site. In the foreground is the London line and the New England Road bridge. The original brick arch of the latter can be seen beyond the lattice structure. It has been subsequently further widened. The early junction signal box and ticket collecting platform can be seen on the right. (D. Cullum collection)

Preston Road and Viaduct, Brighton

13. Soon after noon on 25th May 1943, five bombs were dropped on SR property destroying two arches of the viaduct, killing one railwayman and damaging 55 coaches together with 40 wagons. Power supplies and signalling were also disrupted. (British Rail)

14. This July 1983 view of the same location enables us to use the late Eric Morecambe's phrase "you can't see the join". Even the balustrade was impeccably restored. The trains seen are a 4CAP bound for Seaford; electro-diesel no. 73.138 ready to leave with vans for New Cross and a 4CIG berthed in Lovers Walk sidings – an unusually romantically named railway installation. (J.A.M. Vaughan)

15. The track remained suspended in mid-air, whilst the school building on the left lost only tiles and glass. A temporary steel structure was erected and the adjacent arches braced to enable train services to be resumed. (British Rail)

16. When photographed on 4th August 1943, the replacement brick pier was rising amidst the complexities of the engineer's ingenuity. Mr. Davey's road transport remained debilitated amongst the sanitary fittings in his builder's yard. (British Rail)

17. Periodically Hastings line diesel-electrics have to visit Eastleigh works for repairs. Here we see no. 1012 entering Brighton on 12th March 1983, prior to reversing up to Preston Park and continuing westwards via the Cliftonville spur. Only platform 3 can be approached from any direction and then only by a maximum of four coaches. (J.A.M. Vaughan)

LONDON ROAD

18. No. 2592 of class E5 arrives with a Lewes-bound train at the down platform, although it would have left Brighton alongside an *up* London train. The sidings in the distance and most of the platform awning have disappeared in recent years. The leading van is ex-LBSCR. (Lens of Sutton)

→

20. The staggered platforms are joined by a subway, the footbridge being simply a public right-of-way. The banner repeater signal indicated the position of the home signal at the end of the down platform. The train is entirely composed of ex-SECR equipment, still operating in June 1957, and is seen arriving from Tonbridge. (P. Hay)

19. Behind this enthusiasts special returning from Kemp Town on 23rd June 1956, we can see the junction signals and the 63 yd-long Ditchling Road tunnel. The locomotive chosen for the trip was the Brighton Works shunter no. 377S, which like *Boxhill* earlier, had been repainted in Stroudley's yellow livery. It had started life as no. 35 *Morden* and was scrapped in 1963, as BR no. 32635. (P. Hay)

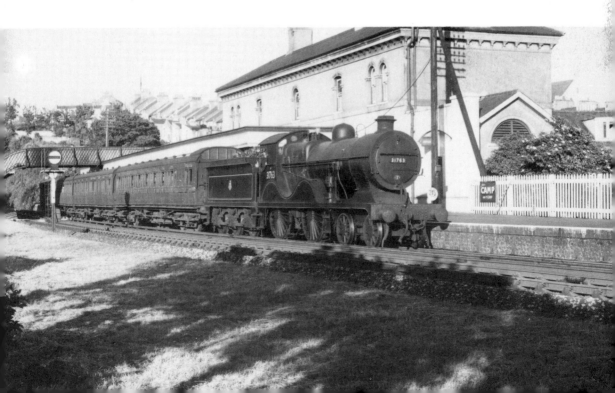

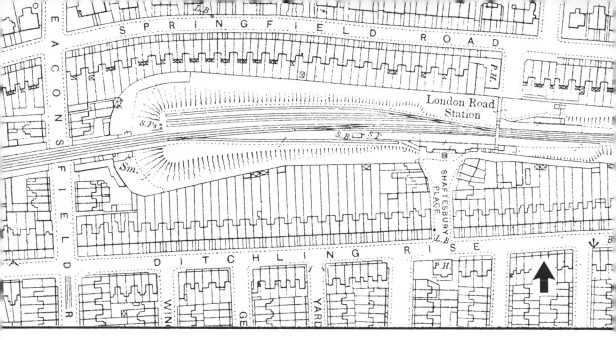

The station was opened on 1st October 1877 and the plans show that it was originally intended to name it Ditchling Rise, which would have been more truthful. This 1911 map shows the revised position of the four carriage sidings and the location of the signal box (SB) and signal posts (SP).

21. This pleasing symmetrical architectural style was employed at Portslade when that station was rebuilt in 1882. We must be thankful that new uses can be found for railway buildings when they cease to be fully utilised, so that this aspect of our heritage is not lost to the demolition contractors. (C. Hall)

KEMP TOWN JUNCTION

22. 23. Two pictures showing the handover of the train staff for the single line to Kemp Town in the early 1950s. The little 19-lever wooden signal box probably dated from the branch opening in 1869, as it is one of the 'stilts' variety. One of the trains is a railtour with a 'Terrier' (A1X class 0–6–0 tank) and a two-coach 'Brighton' motor set. The other is the daily goods behind E4 class no. 32511. The branch was single line throughout by 1953, the other tracks in view being sidings. Notice the massive telegraph poles. When this picture was taken, much of the railway telephone system was carried by omnibus circuits on pole routes, to the great disadvantage of being heard and understood. (Both P. Hay)

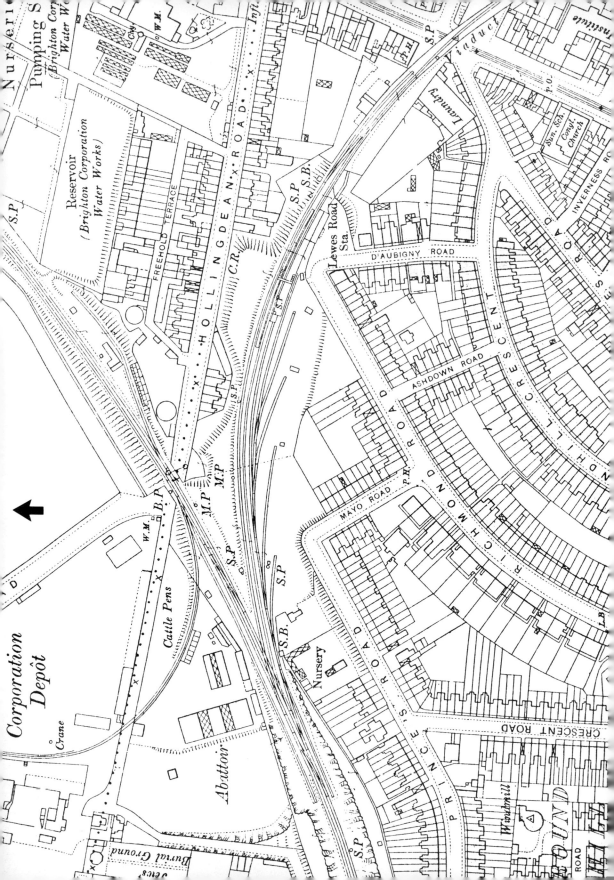

THE KEMP TOWN BRANCH

24. A prospect of eastern Brighton from above Ditchling Road tunnel. Kemp Town Junction is in the foreground with the little signal box just visible. The line on the right goes to Kemp Town, with trucks in the coal yard of Lewes Road station. In the centre is the line from Lewes with a Tonbridge to Brighton train headed by class L no. 31770. To the left of its smoke is the siding to Brighton abattoir, and on the opposite side of the line is the site of the LBSCR gasworks. (P. Hay)

← The line from Brighton appears in a cutting at the bottom of this 1910 map and the initial double track of the branch diverges to the right, past the coal yard. Lewes Road station is shown with a footbridge to the island platform and a signal box at the commencement of the single line section. Note that the single line crosses from one side of the viaduct to the other, whilst passing over the tramway tracks of Lewes Road. On the left of the page is a siding serving the Corporation's refuse destructor and also the abattoir. The siding on the opposite side of the Lewes main line is seen entering the LBSCR gas works, which produced oil gas, used initially for carriage lighting but later only for the dining and Pullman car cookers.

HISTORICAL BACKGROUND

Residential development to the east of the old town of Brighton was commenced in the 1820s by Thomas Kemp and was completed by a number of other property developers. On 2nd August 1869, the 1¼ mile long branch was opened without any intermediate stations. It was a costly line to build, having two viaducts (Lewes Road 14 arches and Hartingon Road 3 arches) and a 1024 yd. long tunnel. The LBSCR seemed to consider the expense justified, if only to prevent a projected rival line from London arriving in the eastern part of Brighton.

Passenger services were withdrawn temporarily between 1st January 1917 and 10th August 1919 and permanently on 1st January 1933. The tunnel was used as an over-night air raid shelter for electric trains (steam hauled) between October 1941 and May 1944, except for the few weeks of the closure of the London Road Viaduct. The terminus continued to act as "Brighton East Goods Depot" until 14th August 1971, during which time it relieved the pressure on the cramped main goods depot.

Bradshaw's 1890 timetable.

Fares.]	BRIGHTON and KEMP TOWN.—London, Brighton, and South Coast.																Sunday.									
1 cl. 2 cl. 3 cl.	Brighton (Central) .... dep	6 50	8	5 9	10 10	10 11	5	11 48	12 35	1	4 52	37 3	30 4	1 55	20 6	10 7	35 8	5 8	40 9	20		8 45 9	40 2	1 55	0 7	3 5	53
0 5 0 20 1	London Road	6 53	8	8 9	13 10	13 11	8	11 51	12 38	1	48 2	40 3	33 4	18 5	23 6	13 7	28 8	8 8	43 9	23		8 48 9	43 2	18 5	3 7	6 8	36
0 5 0 20 1	Lewes Road	6 56	8	11 9	16 10	16 11	11	11 54	12 41	1	51 2	43 3	36 4	21 5	26 6	16 7	31 8	11 8	46 9	26		8 51 9	46 2	21 5	6 7	9 8	39
0 40 30 2	Kemp Town .... arr	7	1 8	16 9	21 10	21 11	16	11 59	12 46	1	56 2	48 3	41 4	26 5	31 6	21 7	36 8	16 8	51 9	31		8 56 9	51 2	26 5	11 7	14 8	44
1 cl. 2 cl. 3 cl.	Kemp Town .... dep	7	15 8	28 9	23 10	49 11	25	12	7 1	0 2	10 2	55 3	45 4	40 5	35 6	40 7	45 8	22 8	55 9	42		8 10 9	5 10	40 2	40 5	30 8	0 8 48
0 5 0 20 1	Lewes Road	7	18 8	31 9	31 10	43 11	28	12	10 1	3 2	13 2	58 3	48 4	43 5	38 6	43 7	48 8	25 8	58 9	45		8 13 9	8 10	43 2	43 5	33 8	3 8 51
0 4 0 30 1½	London Road 72	7	21 8	34 9	34 10	46 11	31	12	13 1	6 2	16 3	1 3	51 4	46 5	41 6	46 7	51 8	28 9	1 9	48		8 16 9	11 10	46 2	46 5	36 8	6 8 54
0 40 30 2	Brighton (Central) 74, 68, 67 arr	7	26 8	39 9	39 10	51 11	36	12	18 1	11 2	21 3	6 3	56 4	51 5	46 6	51 7	56 8	33 9	6 9	53		8 21 9	16 10	51 2	51 5	41 8	11 8 59

25. On 6th July 1969, we see class 09 no. D3720 (later 09.009) passing over the catch points and past the ground signal. The branch was, by then, effectively a siding. Grass was growing up in readiness for the death sentence.
(J.A.M. Vaughan)

LEWES RD CONGREGATIONAL CH. OUTING. 5/7/09.

26. Opened on 1st September 1873, this station was typical of the branch in handling many church parties. The 1932 figures emphasise the point. On the left is the beginning of the viaduct parapet and behind the left canopy stanchion is the covered stairway from the street. (Lens of Sutton)

Party	From	To	Adlts.	Juveniles.	Total
St. Annes S.S.	Kemp Town	Hassocks	20	100	120
The Rev. Streeter	Lewes Rd.	Burgess H.	30	200	230
St. George's S.S.	Kemp Town	Hassocks	30	125	155
Bristol Rd. Meth. S.S.	Kemp Town	Burgess H.	40	80	120
Pelham Inst. S.S.	Kemp Town	Burgess H.	150	200	350
Girls' Guildry Rally.	Kemp Town	Southwick	19	65	84
" " "	Lewes Rd.	"	35	77	112
St. Martins Ch. S.S.	Lewes Rd.	Hassocks	50	270	320
St. Marks S.S.	Kemp Town	Hassocks	50	350	400
Lewes Rd. Congl. S.S.	Lewes Rd.	Hassocks	25	175	200
St. Matthews S.S.	Kemp Town	Burgess H.	12	120	132
Moulscombe S.S.	Lewes Rd.	Hassocks	100	700	800
St. Michaels S.S.	Lewes	Kemp Town	50	110	160

It has been said that the Railway offers the best way to travel in this world and that the Church offers the best way to the next.

27. Looking north in 1952, we see the destructor chimney in the distance and the ramp of the former island platform on the right. The building became a pickle factory and later a builder's store. (R.C. Riley)

28. The goods from Kemp Town is seen passing the coal yard in September 1953, hauled by no. 32165, an E3 with E4 splashers. Traffic was considerable and the curiosities of shunting at Kemp Town resulted in an un fitted brake van in the middle of the train, as well as one at the far end. (P. Hay)

30. A class E4 0–6–2T leaves the viaduct in the background and hauls its train over Hartington Road. A halt of that name, situated to the left of the locomotive, had been in use between 1st January 1906 and April 1911. (P. Hay)

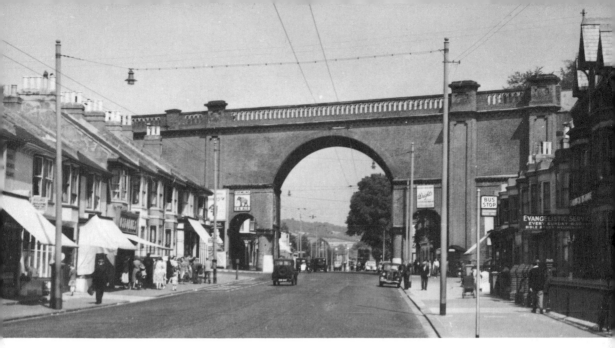

29. Looking north, in 1950, at the now long-lost Lewes Road landmark, we see that the tram tracks had been replaced by trolleybus wires. The tram fare to town had been 1d, but the rail fare was 1½d at the time of closure. (R.C. Riley)

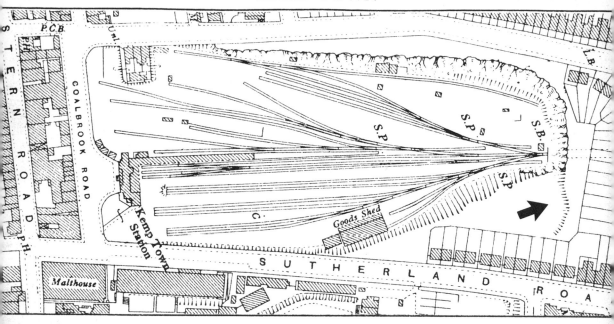

When opened, the station was provided with only four sidings and a platform road. During the 1870s the site was excavated and the yard extended to give a layout similar to the one shown on this 1931 map. A few sidings were removed in 1933 but generally few changes were made before final closure.

31. A train of close-coupled four-wheeled coaches, designed by Stroudley, awaits departure from the station's only platform, around the turn of the century. The locomotive is class D1 no. 28 *Isfield*, which was scrapped in 1912. The smoking chimney was part of the Albion Steam Flour Mills, which provided considerable railway traffic. (E.R. Lacey collection)

33. Initially the signal box was situated on the opposite side of the line. Only this tunnel portal remains today as evidence of railway occupation of what is now an industrial estate. (D. Cullum collection)

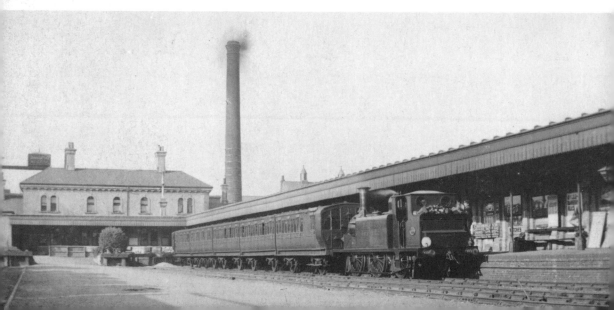

32. Following an unsuccessful experiment with petrol railcars in 1906, the branch was provided with rail motors of the type seen here. At first, the driver controlled the engine mechanically from the end of the coach, but in 1911 a pneumatic system was introduced. In 1931, 50 trips per day were run with a single coach and 20 with two. Note the departing goods train. (Lens of Sutton)

34. When photographed in 1949, the station building was used as the goods office, a coal office and a residence. The similarity of design with London Road and Portslade is worth noting. (T. Middlemass)

Also of note are the annual ticket records:

	Issued	Collected
1925	66529	98558
1926 (General Strike)	45722	65948
1927	50627	69763
1928 (Fares increase)	30594	43047
1929	30864	51487
1930	26205	42384
1931	21429	36270

35. The complexities of the permanent way seldom make the central feature of a railway photograph. This interesting detail was recorded on 23rd June 1956, whilst the SLS Special (seen in photograph nos. 19 and 23) was waiting to return to Brighton.
(A.E. Bennett)

36. The final special train was operated by the Woking Homes Committee on 26th June 1971. As steam had ceased on the Southern Region in 1967, a diesel-electric unit was considered to be the only practical alternative. (S.C. Nash)

37. The hillside location and the deep chalet-style eaves give a distinctly alpine look to the most modern station on the line. How preferable it is to the featureless flat-roofed structures erected elsewhere. It was the first new station on the Southern Region for over 12 years. The first ticket to Falmer reveals the date of opening. (J. Scrace)

38. This drawing appeared in the Illustrated London News on 13th June 1846 and shows the classical balustrading similar to that used on its big brother in Brighton. The turnpike road appears to use two arches. (R. Mitchell collection)

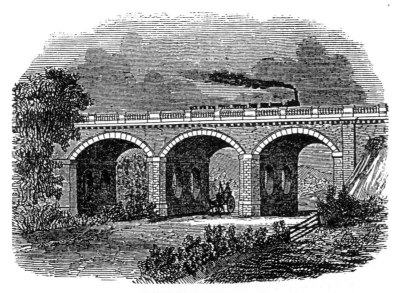

THE HODSHROVE SKEW BRIDGE.

39. With part of the Moulsecoomb Estate as a backdrop, L1 class no. 31787 forges ahead up the bank to Falmer on 22nd April 1956 with the Sundays only 5.51pm Brighton to Charing Cross via Tonbridge, composed of two 'birdcage' sets. Notice the first class saloon in the middle of the second coach, a delightful feature of these sets. About 1910 two of the arches were strengthened by infilling with brick, the highway by then using the central arch only. (P. Hay)

40. A dual carriageway was built in 1967, necessitating reinforcement of the western arch with a concrete bow-string span which, whilst functional, aesthetically imbalances the whole structure. (V. Mitchell)

41. On 26th May 1957, the 1.55 pm Brighton to Tonbridge train was composed of the then usual Birdcage Set and L class 4–4–0. It is seen climbing the 1 in 101 gradient past Falmer Pumping Station. In 1903 the goods yard head shunt was extended to form a siding for conveying coal supplies for the five Lancashire boilers, which provided steam to the two massive triple expansion condensing engines connected to the pumps. WM on the 1911 map indicates weighing machine. The siding was removed in about 1954; steam pumping ceased in 1958 and the pump house was demolished in 1962. (P. Hay)

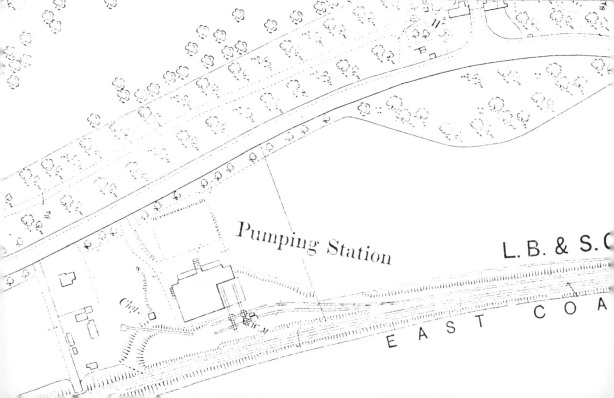

Pumping Station

L. B. & S. C

EAST COA

FALMER

42. The original station was opened on 8th June 1846, on a site about one mile east of the present one. The latter was brought into use on 1st August 1865, and was rebuilt in 1890 but only one goods siding was provided initially, at the east end of the platforms as shown on the 1873 map, overleaf. This explains why the signal box, visible in the distance, was remote from the later goods yard. (P. Hay collection)

1911 map.

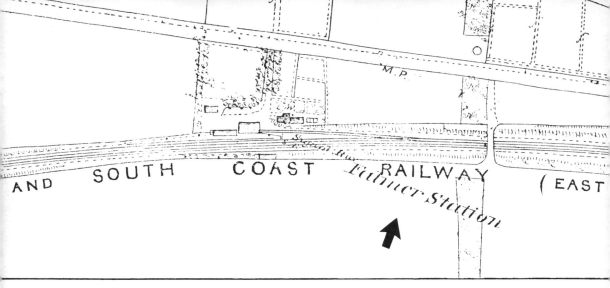

AND   SOUTH   COAST   RAILWAY   (EAST

M.P.

Falmer Station

1873 map.

43. Class D1 0–4–2T no. 2274 drifts in from Brighton on 11th October 1933. The rear bogie of the train is on the connection to the goods yard, which closed in 1961. Note the oil lamps and signal of the period. (H.C. Casserley)

45. A Brighton to Tonbridge train approaching the site of Falmer's original station, on the Lewes side of the tunnel. This first station was inconvenient for both the village and Stanmer House. Today only a slight widening of the shallow cutting sides marks its position. In 1957, steam trains did not stop at Falmer, and the driver of L class no. 31760 has already shut off steam to coast down the 1 in 88 to Lewes. (P. Hay)

44. On the same day, a light engine from Lewes (class E4 no. 2505) coasts down hill, having emerged from the 490 yd. long tunnel just beyond the bridge. The gangers' huts are on the site of the original siding. (H.C. Casserley)

46. When photographed on 27th April 1971, 2HAL unit no. 2656 had not long received its yellow high-visibility front end and matching 1st class bands. Apart from the introduction of electric traction and lighting, the station, which is similar to those on the Oxted-Groombridge line, was little changed. (J. Scrace)

47. The low sun on 3rd December 1983 illuminates the signal box which was installed by the Southern Railway in an extension to the booking office, so that both could be worked by one man. Staffing levels had to be increased with the arrival of the University of Sussex acros the road. The dull flat-roofed up platform waiting room of modern construction was not in use that day as trains from Brighton were terminating here, due to engineering works. (V. Mitchell)

48. The Friars Walk facade of the 1846 terminus was imposingly designed in classical style with massive Corinthian pilasters, tastefully surrounded by yellow brick. It survived until the 1960s, when it was inexcusably destroyed. (T. Middlemass)

49. The chalet style of the second station was much admired by the local press, but the brick infilling of the timber frames would not have encouraged durability. The elaborate effect is enhanced by the ornate ridge tiles, barge boards and lamp bracket. (G. Holmes collection)

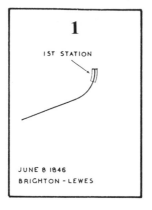

1ST STATION

JUNE 8 1846
BRIGHTON - LEWES

The changes that have occurred to the railway arrangements over the years are so complex that they are best illustrated by diagrams and maps.

Double track was initially laid from Brighton (diag.1) into a terminus at Friars Walk and *within eight weeks* the line, although only single track, was extended towards Hastings (diag.2), making a nonsense of providing a terminus. With the arrival of the more direct line from London (diag.3), the need to run through trains in and out of the station was acutely inconvenient and so some

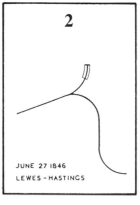

JUNE 27 1846
LEWES - HASTINGS

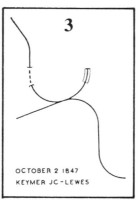

OCTOBER 2 1847
KEYMER JC - LEWES

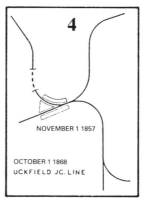

NOVEMBER 1 1857

OCTOBER 1 1868
UCKFIELD JC. LINE

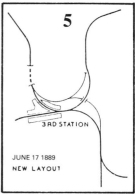

3RD STATION

JUNE 17 1889
NEW LAYOUT

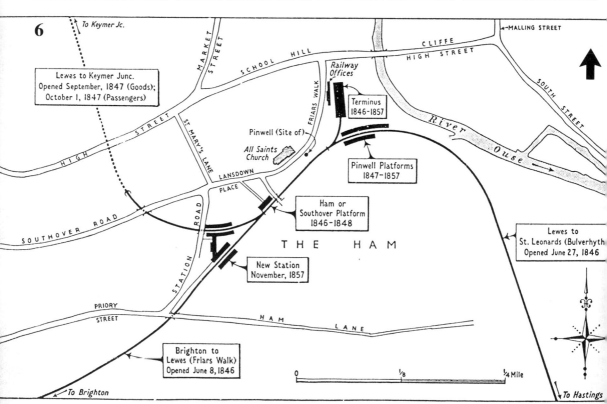

Station arrangements at Lewes, 1846-1857   (Railway Magazine)

temporary and initially unroofed platforms were erected near the junction (diag.6). Double track was brought into use on 30th January 1847 and the Lewes muddle was compounded by the addition of a small platform, without amenities, for the benefit of the residents of Southover. It was used for ticket collecting.

The opening of new routes to Uckfield and Newhaven made operations extremely difficult and eventually, in 1857, a proper junction station was built, together with a new link to the Uckfield line (diag.4). The chairman of the LBSCR described the first station which was only in use for 11 years, as "the most incomplete and injudicious station ever erected".

To increase the number of platforms and reduce the small radius of the curves the second station was rebuilt after only 32 years use.

The third and present station is located a little to the south of its predecessor and was brought into use on 17th June 1889.

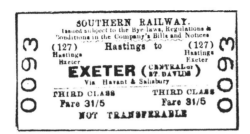

50. The departure platform for Brighton is adjacent to the goods shed in this 1887 view. Note the sturdy locomotive water crane and the ornamental "bed head" style of name board. (National Railway Museum)

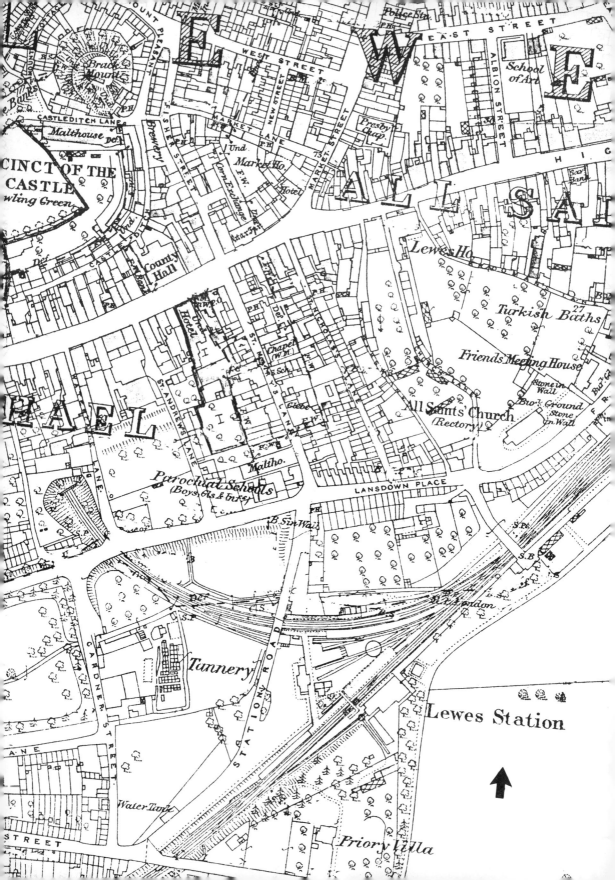

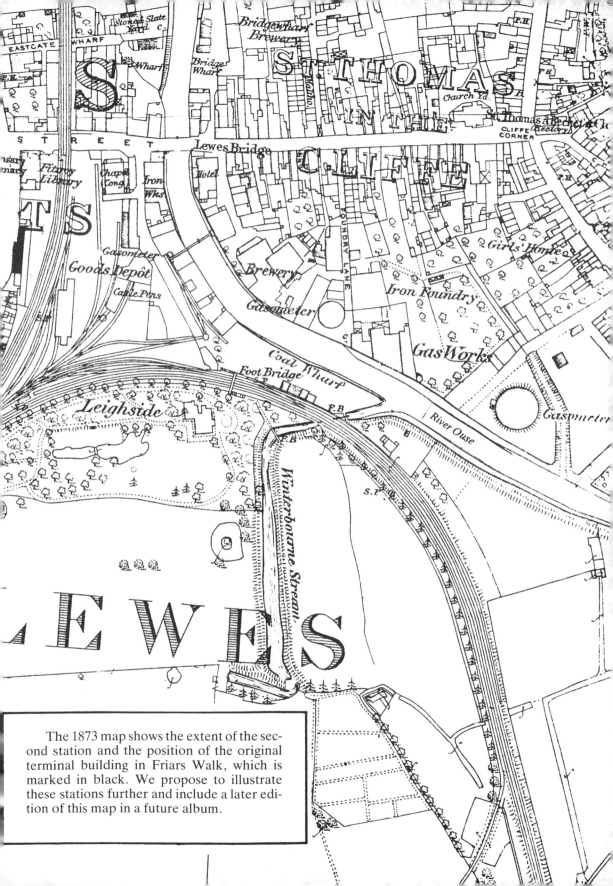

The 1873 map shows the extent of the second station and the position of the original terminal building in Friars Walk, which is marked in black. We propose to illustrate these stations further and include a later edition of this map in a future album.

51. Looking towards Brighton in 1888, the central feature is the once popular train shed, similar to that at Barnham, which is illustrated in the *Worthing to Chichester* album in this series. On the right is the back of the "chalet" seen in photograph 49 and the turntable, an obvious feature on the 1873 map. (National Railway Museum)

→

53. A view from Ham Lane bridge during the widening of the site in preparation for construction of the third station. The structures on the left were seen in picture no. 50. (Lens of Sutton)

52. Looking in the other direction, there are no less than twelve semaphore signals visible. They have slotted posts, into which they disappear when "off" and remote lamps, which rotate. The bridge, with arched approach, was provided to gain access to just one house (*Leighside* – see map) and the goods shed. This bridge was still largely intact in 1984. (E.J. Bedford/R.C. Riley collection)

54. We have many better quality photographs but include this one because it shows a carriage truck *with a carriage on it*. No. 325 *Abergavenny* is one of the G class and was built in 1877. The new station, in the background, was partly built by Longleys, who are still undertaking major building projects in the south of England. (R.C. Riley collection)

55. Some of the staff in 1912 – booking clerks (non-uniformed), ticket collectors, porters, and one signal box lad in the front row left. (G. Holmes collection)

56. A change from the local livery happened twice daily with the passing of the Liverpool train. The London & North Western Railway Company's train had travelled via Brighton where no. 183 *Eastbourne* took it over. It is one of the "Gladstones", built in 1889 and withdrawn in 1929. (E.R. Lacey collection)

57. Another "Gladstone" class BI. This was formerly named *George A Wallis*, who was the first mayor of Eastbourne. Whilst the fireman takes on water, the driver oils the inside motion. Cattle trucks and shunt signals add interest to this quality shot. (O.J. Morris/Lens of Sutton)

58. One of the many D class tanks, no. 273
Dornden, accelerates away with ancient and
modern coaches – four-wheelers and bogies.
(Lens of Sutton)

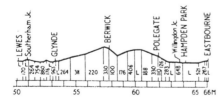

Gradient profile also showing the mileage
from London.

60. Looking in the opposite direction with
the new London up platform in the distance,
we see two more fragments of the earlier
platforms, together with some of the former
down side buildings. (D. Cullum collection)

59. The London lines of the second station were retained when the third station was opened, together with short lengths of disused platform. The nearer bridge is that previously seen in photograph no. 52, whilst the bridge in the distance carried the Uckfield line. It appears that parts of the old signal box were re-used to build a store under the bridge. The retention of these lines enabled goods trains to bypass the new passenger station. (O.J. Morris/E. Jackson collection)

61. No. 2385, of class D3, rumbles over the crossings in front of the junction signal box on 24th October 1934. The ex-LBSCR signal post was known as *The Gallows* and the disc signals, each bearing a white painted hand, rotated to indicate permission to enter sidings. (H.C. Casserley)

The following figures for 1936 indicate the volume of traffic handled :—

Tickets issued (excluding Seasons)	226,500
Seasons issued	3,240
Platform tickets	29,820
Tickets collected (excluding "Platforms")... ...	495,830
Parcels, outwards	13,790
„ inwards	47,180
Milk, outwards, gallons	25,560
„ inwards „	5,280
General Goods, outwards, tons	13,980
„ „ inwards „	13,630
Coal, etc., inwards, tons	33,040
Minerals, outwards, tons	14,540
Wagons loaded, outwards...	4,630
„ „ inwards	11,170
„ transferred	125,810
P.L.A., outwards	1,280
„ inwards	1,270

62. The driver of class E4 0–6–2T no. 2503 adopts a casual pose as the former LBSCR brake van of his Hornby-type goods train passes over the points of the down Uckfield line. Local pick-up trips were worked as far as Plumpton in the east and Glynde in the west. (Lens of Sutton)

63. Class E5 no. 2573 blows off whilst taking water in platform 6. An inclined ramp, visible on the right, was provided for luggage trolleys to the centre platforms, the others having lifts. An assortment of coaches makes up a heavy Tunbridge Wells train on August Bank Holiday 1950. (R.C. Riley)

64. The up boat train from Newhaven cautiously negotiates the junction on 7th August 1950, with an improvised reporting number covering the locomotive number, which was 31904. Boat trains ran non-stop through the station. Very muscular signalmen were required to move this tonnage of point rodding. (R.C. Riley)

65. On 5th November 1960, severe flooding caused cessation of electric services and their substitution by any steam available, such as this class U1 2–6–0. It has been reported that the Borough Surveyor wished to reduce the impounding of water to the west of the station by blowing up the London platforms but the BR District Engineer declined to co-operate. It could have been a novel addition to the famous and elaborate Lewes Bonfire Night. (E. Wilmshurst)

66. The 4COR units were built for use mainly on the two routes from London to Portsmouth and hence earned the nickname *Pompeys*. A few of them spent their final years on East Coast services. This example is seen in 1970, fitted with roller blinds in place of the original stencil numbers.
(J.A.M. Vaughan)

67. An Ore to Brighton train leaves platform 7 on 5th April 1983. The white tower houses the luggage lift. Extension of platform 6 was undertaken after platforms 4 and 5 were taken out of use. Note the white painted bridge spanning the track bed and the vaulted roof covering the large area between platforms 3 and 4. (J. Scrace)

69. In addition to the goods yard close to the town, there were eleven sidings in the East Yard capable of holding an average of 36 wagons each. Although poorly illuminated, we see class C2 0–6–0 no. 555, built in 1902, bound for Newhaven, passing the site of one of the last avalanches in the south. During a typical 24 hours in 1911, goods trains worked thus – 26 departures, 25 arrivals and 7 passing. (E.R. Lacey collection)

London Brighton & South Coast Railway

Rotherfield to

Chichester

←

68. The lantern roof, the octagonal ornaments and the heavily keyed arches combine to give an unusual and interesting appearance, despite the loss of the large vaulted canopy over the pavement. (C. Hall)

70. One of the elegant ex-LBSCR class L 4–6–4 tanks, no. 2328, at the same location as the previous picture, photographed on 24th April 1935. The Pullman Car and the following two coaches are crossing the River Ouse, on Southerham Bridge. The quarry and chimney is that of Eastwoods Cement Works. (S.W. Baker)

The 1910 map shows the lime works of G. Newington & Co which soon after became the Lewes Portland Cement Co. Eastwoods took over in 1929 and closed the works in 1981.

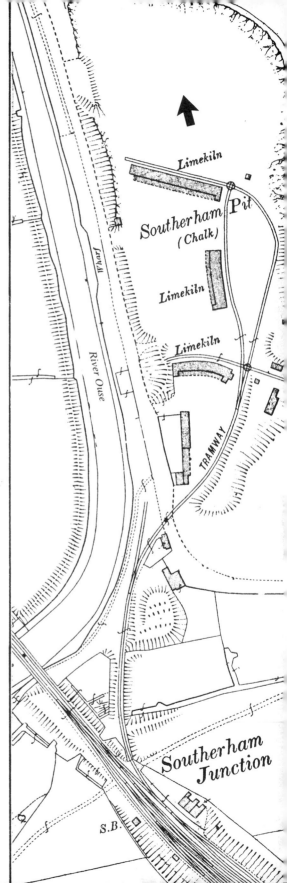

72. Cement Works motive power in 1955 was this Andrew Barclay saddle tank (No. 919 of 1902). Later Hawthorn Leslie 0–4–0ST *Atlas* was in use until replaced by a diesel. Earlier, in 1935, the works locomotive was used in an attempt to free a grounded barge, but only succeeded in falling into the river itself. (S.C. Nash)

71. During the early 1930s the only commercial traffic on the River Ouse was cement from Lewes to Newhaven Harbour and on 5th April 1935 a wayward cement barge damaged one of the steel piers of the opening bridge. It required a gang of over 30 men to roll the bridge back for the occasional passage of a barge and so an agreement was reached whereby cement would be taken to Newhaven by rail *free of charge* if the operation could be eliminated. A new concrete pier was built to encase the damaged steel work and it can be seen here under "Schools" class *Merchant Taylor*. The construction equipment is visible in the previous photograph. The train engine of the Up Boat Train on 13th April 1958 was ex-SECR class L no. 31776. (R.C. Riley)

73. Eastwood's diesel locomotive conveys a BR standard 16-ton mineral wagon across the A27 on 5th September 1975. The cement works site is now an industrial estate; BR no longer uses loose coupled wagons and the A27 now bypasses the area. Time marches on! (J. Scracc)

75. The 23-lever signal box was closed on 18th September 1976 and the control of the junction transferred to a panel in the remaining box at Lewes. At about this time the parallel tracks, seen more clearly in the previous photograph, were eliminated. The point of divergence was moved to the south end of the cutting and a new bridge built over it for the rerouted A27, at the the north end. Electro-diesel no. 73138 is seen hauling a Brighton to Newhaven freight on 5th September 1975. (J. Scrace)

London Brighton & South Coast Railway

Chichester to

Hellingly

74. During the prolonged ASLEF strike of 1955, a skeleton service was operated by the few NUR drivers. This 4.05 pm Three Bridges to Hastings train on 4th June 1955 was hauled by BR class 2 no. 41317. The Seaford branch is in the foreground. (S.C. Nash)

76. A 1917 post card shows the mill on the right and the Trevor Arms in the background. The station buildings are little changed today, having been extended in 1874 at a cost of £895. (Lens of Sutton)

77. In LBSCR days, passengers were well protected from adverse weather, even when crossing the footbridge. The photograph shows another pleasing staff parade, complete with the inevitable giant milk churns, so much part of the bygone railway scene. (Lens of Sutton)

The following report is reproduced by courtesy of the Railway Correspondence and Travel Society and is part of an account of problems faced by the Motive Power Dept.

Fireman disappears.

Even more unusual were the happenings of 2nd December, 1913 when No. 373 was working empty stock from Brighton to Hastings for transfer to the South Eastern & Chatham Railway. Driver Ferguson and his young fireman, Harry Williams, were not on the best of terms and apparently had not spoken to each other for some days. Ferguson was near retiring age and recently had been removed from the top link at Brighton because of failing health, so it was not surprising that a much younger man with plenty of energy and new ideas roused his anger and dislike. The sidings at Brighton were left at 9.47 p.m. with a train of thirteen S.E & C.R. six-wheelers and a bogie brake van, and Lewes was reached in due course, where water was taken during a stay of over an hour awaiting the arrival of a horsebox. It was, therefore, 11.32 p.m. before the journey recommenced and Ferguson was feeling the strain of a long spell on the footplate for he had signed on for light duties at 2.10 p.m. By Glynde he had dozed off leaning against the cab side and noticing this at once, Williams decided to have his own back by playing a trick on his unsuspecting partner. So opening the doors on his side of the cab, he placed his cap, sweat rag and shovel on the floor boards to suggest he had inadvertently fallen overboard. Next he clambered along the running plate, round the smokebox and back to Ferguson's side of the engine where he tapped the lookout window until the old man awoke with a start. Looking round and finding the footplate untenanted, he immediately jumped to the expected conclusion and applied the brakes, but in his dazed state forgot that the train was vacuum fitted and panicked when the speed was not immediately reduced. So, not realising his error, he whistled the guard for an emergency stop and reversed the engine which brought the train to such a ragged stop that the couplings between the 5th and 6th coaches parted. After a hurried consultation, the guard ran to protect the rear of the train with detonators while Ferguson walked the half mile to Polegate signal box for help and Williams crept away from the engine to hide in a ditch until it was clear for a dash back along the track to where he could lie down and pretend to be injured. As soon as the guard had retreated to his van Williams made haste through the lineside fields until he calculated it was safe to return to the track. Unfortunately his luck was out for a local poacher was on the run and as he passed Williams he thrust a brace of pheasants into his arms before disappearing into the darkness, where he froze in some bushes leaving Williams to crash around in confusion until gathered up by three keepers and marched off to the police station. Back at the train, assistance eventually arrived and the carriages were stabled for the night at Polegate, but the mystery of the missing fireman was only solved in the morning in the magistrate's court. Williams was acquitted with a severe warning only to find the Company awaiting a full explanation of his conduct the previous evening. The truth could not be hidden and once the whole story was unravelled, Ferguson was placed on the retired list as being unfit for engine driving, while Williams was dismissed the Company's service.

78. To reduce train headway, an intermediate signal box at Ripe crossing, 2¼ miles to the east, was opened in 1899. It was replaced with automatic half barriers in 1965, as was Selmeston crossing. Glynde box ceased to be used on 1st March 1970. The up local on 5th October 1932 was hauled by class E4 no. 2471. (H.C. Casserley)

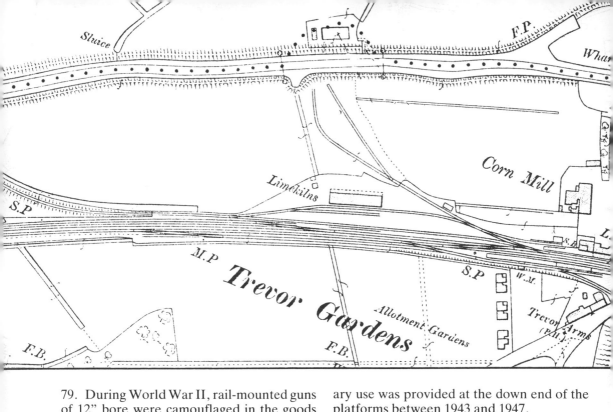

79. During World War II, rail-mounted guns of 12" bore were camouflaged in the goods yard. Owing to the limitations of the road bridge, an emergency level crossing for military use was provided at the down end of the platforms between 1943 and 1947. (British Rail)

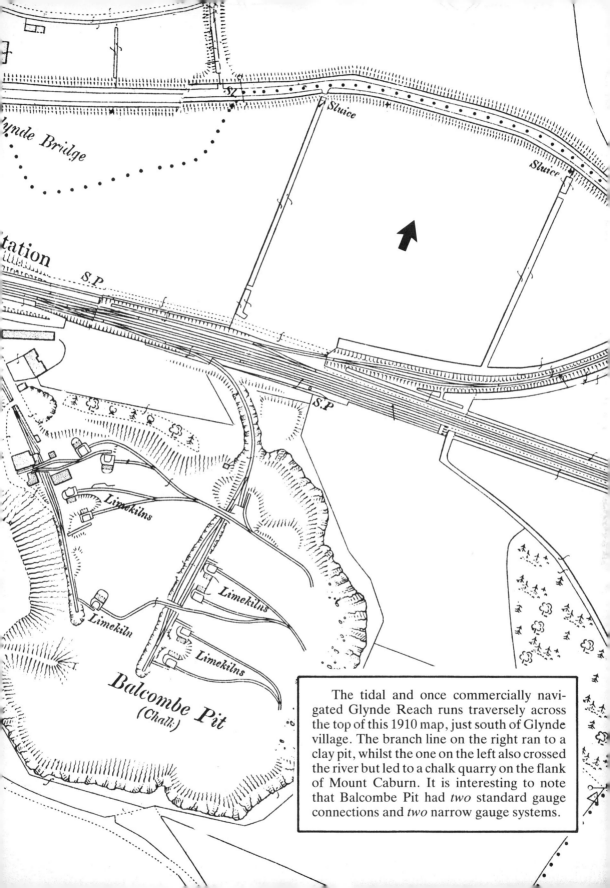

lynde Bridge

Sluice

Sluice

Sluice

tation

S.P

S.P

Limekilns

Limekiln

Limekilns

Limekiln

Limekilns

Balcombe Pit
(Chalk.)

The tidal and once commercially navigated Glynde Reach runs traversely across the top of this 1910 map, just south of Glynde village. The branch line on the right ran to a clay pit, whilst the one on the left also crossed the river but led to a chalk quarry on the flank of Mount Caburn. It is interesting to note that Balcombe Pit had _two_ standard gauge connections and _two_ narrow gauge systems.

80. In 1968 the road bridge was rebuilt. The old and the new abutments can be seen on the right. The circular signal is a banner repeater, introduced by the Southern Railway at loca- tions of limited visibility. The earlier solution was often to erect a signal on a very tall post. (Lens of Sutton)

81. Electric locomotive no. 20002 (ex-SR no. CC2) hums past the electric sub-station on 26th August 1950, at the head of the 12.55 Eastbourne to Manchester train. (S.C. Nash)

→

83. A casual scene outside the *Fullers Arms* as the arrival of a down train is awaited and the carters consume their liquid lunch. Many local people still use the pronunciation – Burr-wick. (Lens of Sutton)

BERWICK

Looking West, Berwick Station, Sussex.

82. An undated post card can capture a moment from the past so well – the dirt road; the LBSCR crossing and wicket gates; the heavily laden passengers, unaware of the camera; the oil lamps. (Lens of Sutton)

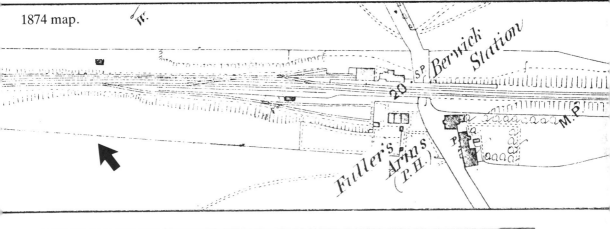

1874 map.

84. The 3.30 pm Eastbourne to Lewes was another unusual steam working during the 1955 ASLEF strike. The sleeper-built gangers' hut, the loading gauge and nearby shunting bell plunger are now almost entirely part of history, although once features of nearly every country station. (S.C. Nash)

85. In 1984, the station still retained its buildings, signal box and signals as illustrated, although the gates were replaced by barriers in 1963. Only one down siding remained in place and that was taken out of use in 1964. A crossover had been retained for emergency use. (Lens of Sutton)

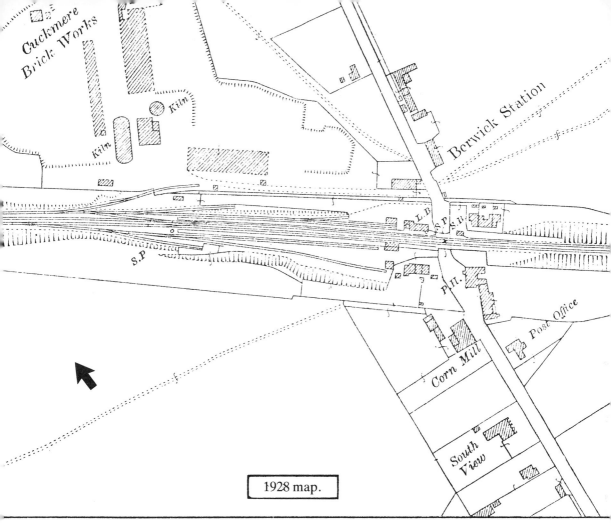

1928 map.

86. Wilmington Crossing is about half way between Berwick and Polegate and made an odd subject for a post card. Travellers on this country road are nowadays protected by the ubiquitous automatic half-barriers. (J.D. Knight collection)

POLEGATE

87. Most of the first station buildings survived until the 1960s. The structure nearest the road was probably from 1846 and was similar to Berwick station. The extension, with semi-dormers, is thought to date from 1849. The lock-up goods warehouse (built in 1893) is in the background of this 1930s view, taken from the signal box.
(O.J. Morris/J. Minnis)

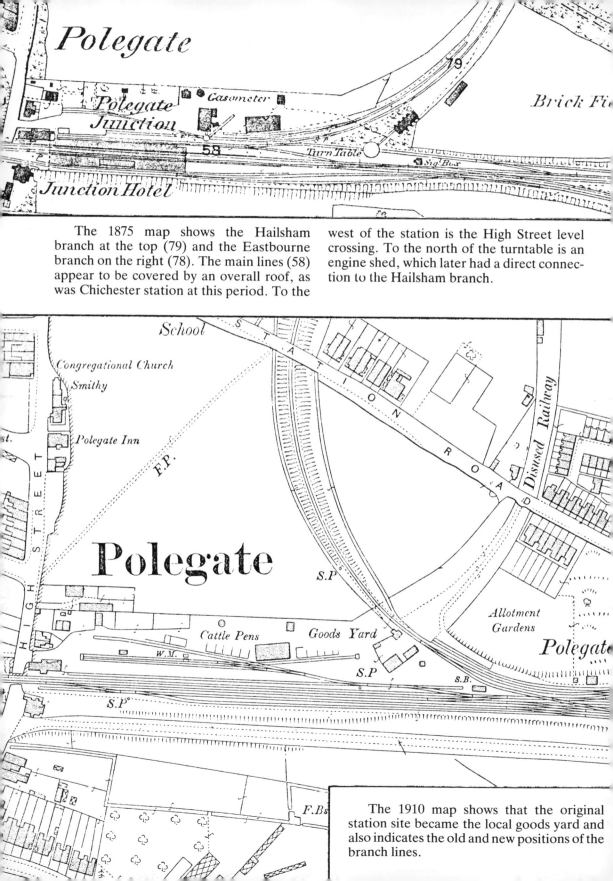

Polegate

Polegate Junction

Gasometer

Junction Hotel

Turn Table

Sig. Box

Brick Fie

79

58

The 1875 map shows the Hailsham branch at the top (79) and the Eastbourne branch on the right (78). The main lines (58) appear to be covered by an overall roof, as was Chichester station at this period. To the west of the station is the High Street level crossing. To the north of the turntable is an engine shed, which later had a direct connection to the Hailsham branch.

School

Congregational Church

Smithy

Polegate Inn

F.P.

HIGH STREET

Polegate

Cattle Pens

W.M.

Goods Yard

S.P.

S.P.

S.P.

Allotment Gardens

Polegate

Disused Railway

STATION ROAD

S.B.

F.Bs

The 1910 map shows that the original station site became the local goods yard and also indicates the old and new positions of the branch lines.

88. Following the re-direction of the Hailsham branch, an entirely new station was
built. The two island platforms were connected by subway to a two-storey building
seen on the left. (R.C. Riley collection)

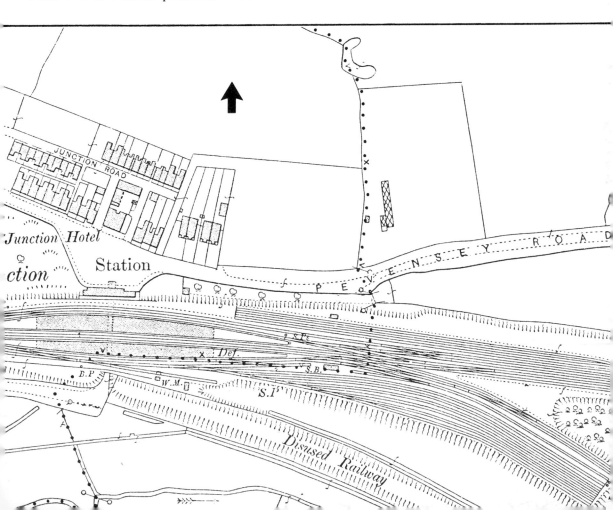

89. The view from the West signal box of four trains, with the Lewes lines in the right foreground. The goods train is headed by class C3 0–6–0 no. 302 which was built in 1906 and survived until 1952. (Lens of Sutton)

90. A train from Eastbourne eases round the last curve on the branch as it passes the East Box, in the days before ballasting over the sleepers was prohibited. It could conceal defective timbers! (Lens of Sutton)

91. Brick, iron and timber structures with lean-to, pitched and curved roofs gave rich variety to the passengers' southern vista in 1945. The grounded coach body passed as a staff mess room – no wonder it was so called – and the slate roof covered the weighing machine of the wagon weighbridge.
(British Rail)

92. A Tunbridge Wells West train heads towards Eastbourne, on 30th July 1949. The exhaust of no. 32028 (class I3) is clearer than the cirrus adorned sky. Note the lack of BR emblem and the up road flange oilers.
(S.C. Nash)

93. The train in the down main platform is the Reading South to Hastings excursion on 16th July 1950, the locomotive being class U1 no. 31896. The up main platform is occupied by two 2BILs on a stopping service. (S.C. Nash)

95. Looking east from the steps of the west or 'A' signal box, class E4 no. 32468 leaves with a train up the 'Cuckoo' line. It is departing from the down loop, with the main lines in the centre of the picture. On the right is the up loop with its starting signals beside another E4, which is standing in No. 2 siding. The lower of the signals controls entry to the 'Cuckoo' line (to Hailsham, Heathfield, etc.); the higher one, with Polegate Crossing signal box distant beneath, applies from the up loop to the up main via the crossover on the extreme right of the picture. Complex as this layout may appear, it had in fact been simplified before 1959 when this picture was taken. (P. Hay)

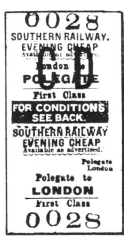

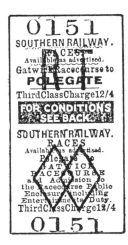

94. In times past, the railways of Britain operated *dozens* of theatrical specials *every Sunday* to convey the props, costumes, scenery and sometimes the performers of the travelling companies. By the time the former LSWR class M7 no. 30053 plodded past 'A' Box with one such special on 13th May 1956, road haulage had secured most of the traffic. (S.C. Nash)

96. An unusual visitor on 26th June 1960 was this ex-SECR P class 0–6–0T. It was on its way from Ashford Works, where it had been repainted, to Sheffield Park, to be preserved and named *Bluebell*. (S.C. Nash)

97. Passenger trains ceased to run through to Tunbridge Wells on 14th June 1965, but continued to operate as far as Hailsham until 9th September 1968, four days after this photograph was taken. Diesel-electric set no. 1119, bound for Eastbourne, forms the 15.49 from Hailsham. (J. Scrace)

98. The direct route to Hastings was officially closed on 6th January 1969 and the up line was lifted soon after. The down line remained and was used occasionally by departmental trains, as on 23rd February 1969 when D6575 and D6566 hauled a long permanent way train from Bexhill to Three Bridges into the down main platform. The junction at Polegate was removed in 1974, the line remaining as a mile long engineer's siding, with access from the east end only, until lifted in August 1984. (S.C. Nash)

99. The entrance and platform canopies have gone and the station has become one of the most dilapidated in the South, as plans are made to build a third station on the site of the first. (C. Hall)

HAMPDEN PARK

100. After prolonged campaigning, local residents finally obtained a station on 1st January 1888. Similar delays occurred at Fittleworth and a station in the same style was built there in the following year (see our *Branch Lines to Midhurst*). Initially named Willingdon, it was renamed on 1st July 1903, as housing development had taken place on Lord Hampden's land. (Lens of Sutton)

101. Due to engineering work at Eastbourne on 1st November 1959, trains terminated here. We see a 12-coach PAN/PUL formation waiting to return to London, with the Pullman car attendant standing on the up platform, whilst a train from Hastings waits to use the crossover. (S.C. Nash)

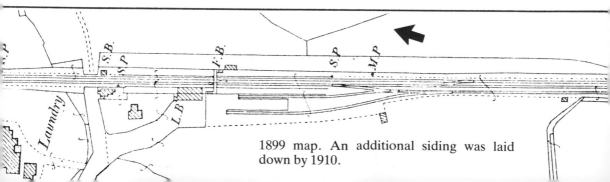

1899 map. An additional siding was laid down by 1910.

102. BR's final steam excursion in Sussex was the Southern Counties Rail Tour on 19th March 1967. It visited Brighton and Eastbourne, concluding with a non-stop run to Victoria. Pacific no. 34108 *Wincanton* is seen from the public footbridge on the down journey. (S.C. Nash)

103. Willingdon Junction is where the Lewes and Hastings lines diverge. It is ½ mile north of Hampden Park signal box which, when the junction box closed in 1930, took control of that part of the route. It now controls lifting barriers instead of gates. An example of the 4COR stock is preserved on the Nene Valley Railway. (C. Hall)

EASTBOURNE

The site of the first station is marked on this 1876 map with an asterisk. The first engine shed had been a two-road building and was situated to the west of the goods shed.

104. The first station was timber built and when it became redundant in 1866 it was removed to the west side of the goods yard where it became a desirable dwelling – no. 1, Wharf Road. For many years it was occupied by railway families and was used as a furniture store in the 1950s. (East Sussex County Library)

105. The second station was altered in 1872 and substantially rebuilt in 1886 to the form seen in this later post card. The vaulted canopy and lantern roof were larger and more elaborate than at Lewes.
(Lens of Sutton)

106. Both pairs of platforms were unhelpfully marked MAIN LINE & BRANCHES and were confusingly numbered from left to right 3 & 4 and 1 & 2! The profusion of advertisements could have only added to the harassed traveller's bewilderment.
(Lens of Sutton)

107. The through train to Liverpool became known as the Sunny South Express and is seen here, on 1st March 1905, ready to depart for Brighton. An oil gas tank wagon can just be seen, beyond the solitary coach.
(Lens of Sutton)

108. One of the popular D class 0–4–2 tanks, no. 267 *Maresfield*, built in 1882, arrives with a medley of ageing four-wheelers. The conical tower bears the words Eastbourne Electric Light Works.
(E.R. Lacey collection)

THROUGH EXPRESS TRAIN SERVICE

BETWEEN

MANCHESTER (Piccadilly)
SHEFFIELD (Victoria)
WALSALL
BIRMINGHAM (New Street)
NOTTINGHAM (Victoria)
COVENTRY
LEICESTER (Central)
RUGBY (Central)

AND

BRIGHTON
EASTBOURNE
with connections for
BEXHILL (Central)
and
HASTINGS

NORTH TO SOUTH

		Fridays only	Saturdays only
		Through Train Manchester (Piccadilly) to Eastbourne 17th July to 14th August	Through Train Walsall to Eastbourne 18th July to 22nd August
Manchester (Piccadilly)	dep	pm 10A25	am ..
Guide Bridge	,,	10 35	..
Sheffield (Victoria)	,,	11A26	..
Walsall	,,	..	10E47
Birmingham (New Street)	,,	..	11F18
Coventry	,,	..	11 50
Nottingham (Victoria)	,,	am 12BS38	..
Loughborough (Central)	,,	12S59	..
Leicester (Central)	,,	1S18	..
Rugby (Central)..	,,	1S47	pm
Brighton	arr	5S18	3 33
Seaford	,,	7SC3	4J21
Eastbourne..	,,	6S 2	4 22
Polegate	,,	6SH52	..
Bexhill (Central)	,,	6SH44	4H53
St. Leonards (Warrior Square)	,,	6SH51	5H 2
Hastings	,,	6SH53	5H 4

SOUTH TO NORTH

		Saturdays only	Saturdays only
		Through Train Eastbourne to Walsall 18th July to 22nd August	Through Train Eastbourne to Manchester (Piccadilly) 18th July to 15th August
Hastings	dep	am 10H44	pm 12H15
St. Leonards (Warrior Square)	,,	10H46	12H17
Bexhill (Central)	,,	10H54	12H24
Eastbourne..	,,	11A25	1A 5
Polegate	,,	..	1C 0
Seaford	,,	11F23	12C47
Brighton	,,	pm 12A15	1A54
Rugby (Central)..	arr	..	5 31
Leicester (Central)	,,	..	5 55
Loughborough (Central)	,,	..	6 15
Nottingham (Victoria)	,,	..	6D35
Coventry	,,	3 53	..
Birmingham (New Street)	,,	4 26	..
Walsall	,,	4 51	..
Sheffield (Victoria)	,,	..	7 54
Guide Bridge	,,	..	8 47
Manchester (Piccadilly)	,,	..	8 57

A—Seats may be reserved, at a fee of 2/- per seat upon personal or postal request to the Station Master. Early application is advisable.
B—Connecting service available from Derby Friargate dep 11 35 pm, Ilkeston North dep 11 53 pm, Kimberley East dep 12 3 am.
C—Change at Brighton
D—Connecting service available to Kimberley East arr 7 2 pm, Ilkeston North arr 7 12 pm, and Derby Friargate arr 7 31 pm.
E—Note "A" applies except on 25th July and 1st August.
F—Change at Lewes and Brighton.
H—Change at Eastbourne.
J—Change at Brighton and Lewes.
S—Saturday mornings 18th July to 15th August.

1964

109. At first glance it appears to be a steam crane. The crane is in fact being hand cranked whilst a shunting engine and cattle truck stand in the background. (E.R. Lacey collection)

110. The 72-lever signal box remains in use today but all the other features have gone. It would now seem unusual to have distant signals immediately outside a terminus. The lower arms indicated whether or not the lines were clear through to the buffer stops. The locomotive is class B1 no. 177. (Lens of Sutton)

111. Until 1911 locomotives were housed in this semi-roundhouse, which was actually only one quarter of a circle. Look for the dumb buffers on the wagon; the white-painted stone (or coal?) by the buffer stops; the pot plant and the brilliant chimney cap on Terrier no. 65 *Tooting*. This locomotive was withdrawn in February 1901, which helps date the photograph. (D. Cullum collection)

Cheap Pleasure Trip Tickets
WILL BE ISSUED AS UNDER
From EASTBOURNE

By Trains leaving at		TO	Return Fares.			
Weekday.	**Sunday.**		1st Class.		3rd Class.	
			s.	d.	s.	d.
9.52, 10.50 a.m.,	9.34, 10.20 a.m.,	HAMPDEN PARK ...	0	7	0	4
1.46, 2.48 p.m.	2.0 p.m.	POLEGATE	1	1	0	7
9.52, 10.50 a.m.,	9.34, 10.20 a.m.,	HAILSHAM	1	11	1	1
12.45, 2.48 p.m.	2.0 p.m.					
		HELLINGLY	2	4	1	4
9.52 a.m.,		WALDRON and HOREHAM ROAD	3	5	1	10
12.45 p.m.	10.20 a.m.	HEATHFIELD	4	0	2	3
		TUNBRIDGE WELLS	7	11	4	4
9.52 a.m.,		BERWICK	2	1	1	3
1.46 p.m.	—	GLYNDE	3	3	1	11
		LEWES	4	0	2	4
3.20 p.m.	10.4 a.m.	SEAFORD	6	4	3	8
		BRIGHTON	6	2	3	6

Available to return by any Train on day of issue only.

Tickets and other information can also be obtained at Messrs. PICKFORDS' Offices, 4, Terminus Buildings, Terminus Road, Eastbourne.

London Bridge Terminus, November. 1922.

WILLIAM FORBES,
General Manager.

1910 map.

112. The scene on 14th March 1944 during repairs to bomb damage. Eastbourne was attacked very frequently and during a raid on 16th September 1942 railwaymen were ironically killed whilst *practising* the use of a fire pump. (British Rail)

114. One of the faithful class E4s, no. 32468, passes along platform 2 with a 1911 ex-LBSCR motor set, in May 1958, on its way to the Hailsham line. In the background, the South Downs rise towards Beachy Head. (P. Hay)

113. In 1911, a new locomotive shed was built ½ mile north of the station and connected to it by a line running parallel to the main lines. It was built on land purchased for the erection of a carriage works. Owing to local objections, the works were built at Lancing instead. The shed had seven straight roads, all leading to a 60ft turntable. In SR days, it was the location of an experimental pulverised fuel plant. When photographed in 1950, bomb damage to the shed had been largely repaired, but it housed few locomotives compared with pre-electrification days. (S.C. Nash)

115. On 19th August 1981, the 10.47 from Walsall arrived behind N class no. 31859 whilst a BR built 2–6–4T shunts in the carriage sidings. Whitley Road coal sidings, on the right, were closed in May 1983 and at the same time rationalisation of the carriage sidings was completed, together with the erection of a carriage washing plant. (S.C. Nash)

116. The extent of the goods yard and cab road roof become apparent from this angle. No. 47105 stands at the head of a Swansea train in platform 4 whilst a 12-coach Victoria train stands in no. 3. A set of HAPs are stabled in the middle road whilst a 4VEP arrives at platform 2 on 22nd May 1979. (S.C. Nash)

117. Much of the original elegance has been retained. One can still admire the fine brick and stone work of the clock tower and the intricate tracery of the canopy stanchion brackets for example. (C. Hall)

118. From the east forecourt on 11th April 1977, we see no. 33062, having brought in a Wolverhampton excursion, and 4CIG no. 7405 berthed in no. 4 station siding. On the following day, the siding and forecourt were taken out of use. Platform 4 was shortened to an 8-car length and the canopy cut back to make way for the construction of a ring road. (S.C. Nash)

119. Locomotive hauled trains have now become a rarity. In this northward view, we see a Chartex Special from the London Midland Region arriving behind no. 33038 on 1st April 1983. The gates in the staggered fence once gave access to private sidings. The many such sidings and the fascinating Crumbles line will be included in the next album in this Series. (J.A.M. Vaughan)

120. One of the now familiar "Gatwick Express" trains appeared briefly on 24th April 1984 on passenger evaluation trials, prior to introduction the following month on their regular route. At the front is a driving brake luggage van (GLV) and at the back is electro-diesel no. 73142 *Broadlands*. Seldom have Eastbourne passengers had the benefit of multi-lingual warning signs that include Chinese. (S.C. Nash)

Other Books from Middleton Press

BRANCH LINE SERIES
Vic Mitchell and Keith Smith
BRANCH LINES TO MIDHURST
BRANCH LINES TO HORSHAM
BRANCH LINE TO SELSEY
BRANCH LINES TO EAST GRINSTEAD
BRANCH LINES TO ALTON
BRANCH LINE TO HAYLING
BRANCH LINE TO SOUTHWOLD

SOUTH COAST RAILWAY SERIES
Vic Mitchell and Keith Smith
BRIGHTON TO WORTHING
WORTHING TO CHICHESTER
CHICHESTER TO PORTSMOUTH

OTHER BOOKS
INDUSTRIAL RAILWAYS OF THE SOUTH-EAST
Chalk Pits Museum
GREEN ROOF OF SUSSEX
Charles Moore
MIDHURST TOWN – THEN AND NOW
Vic and Barbara Mitchell
STEAMING THROUGH KENT
Peter Hay